MANDRILL

RED PANDA

GOLDEN SNUB NOSED MONKEY

SLOTH

BLUE DART FROG

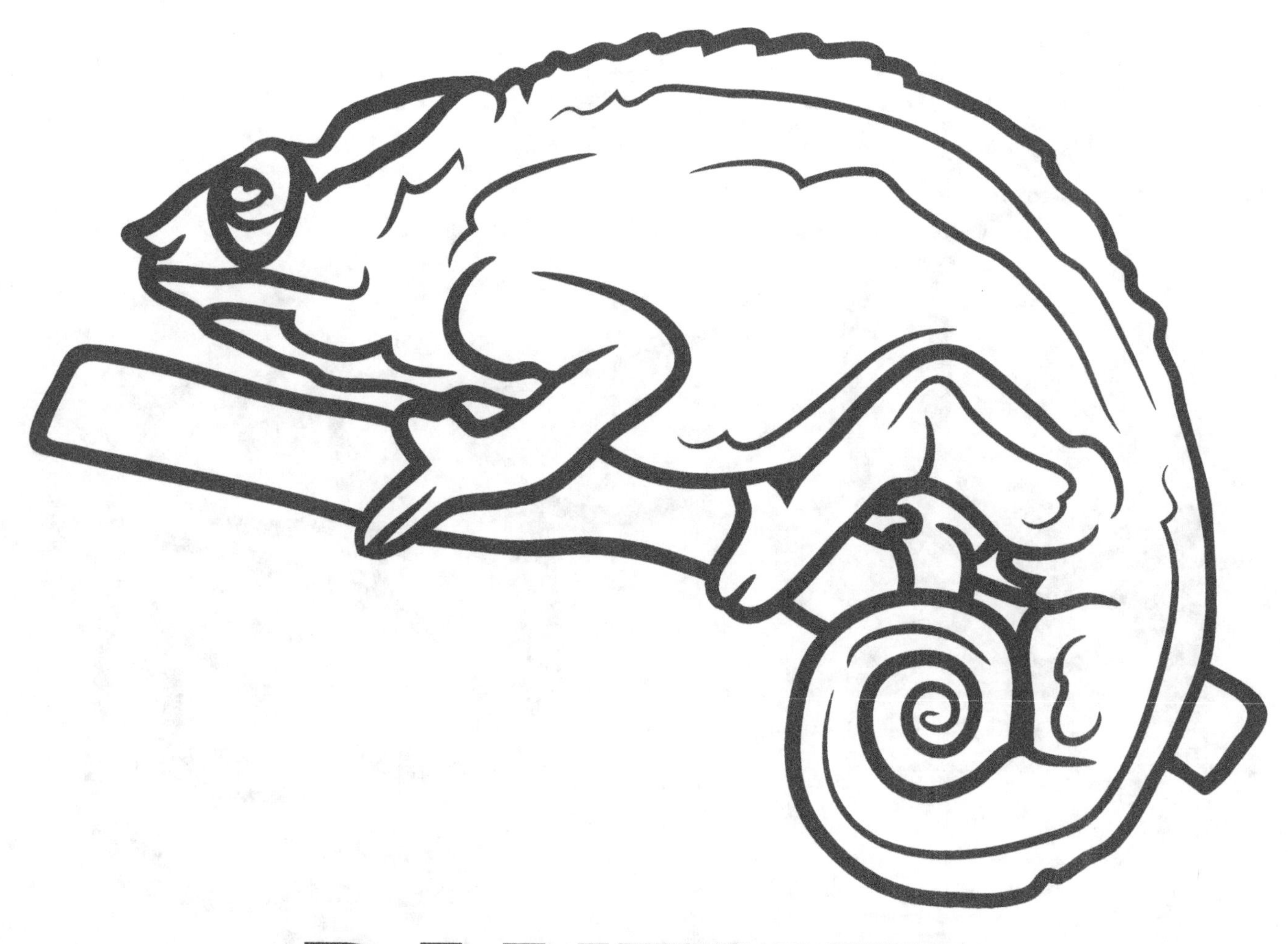

PANTHER

CHAMELEON

EMERALD

TREE BOA

BLUE RACER

CALIFORNIA RED SIDED GARTER SNAKE

RAINBOW BOA

POISON DART FROG

AGAMA LIZARD

Common collared lizard

BLUE MORPHO

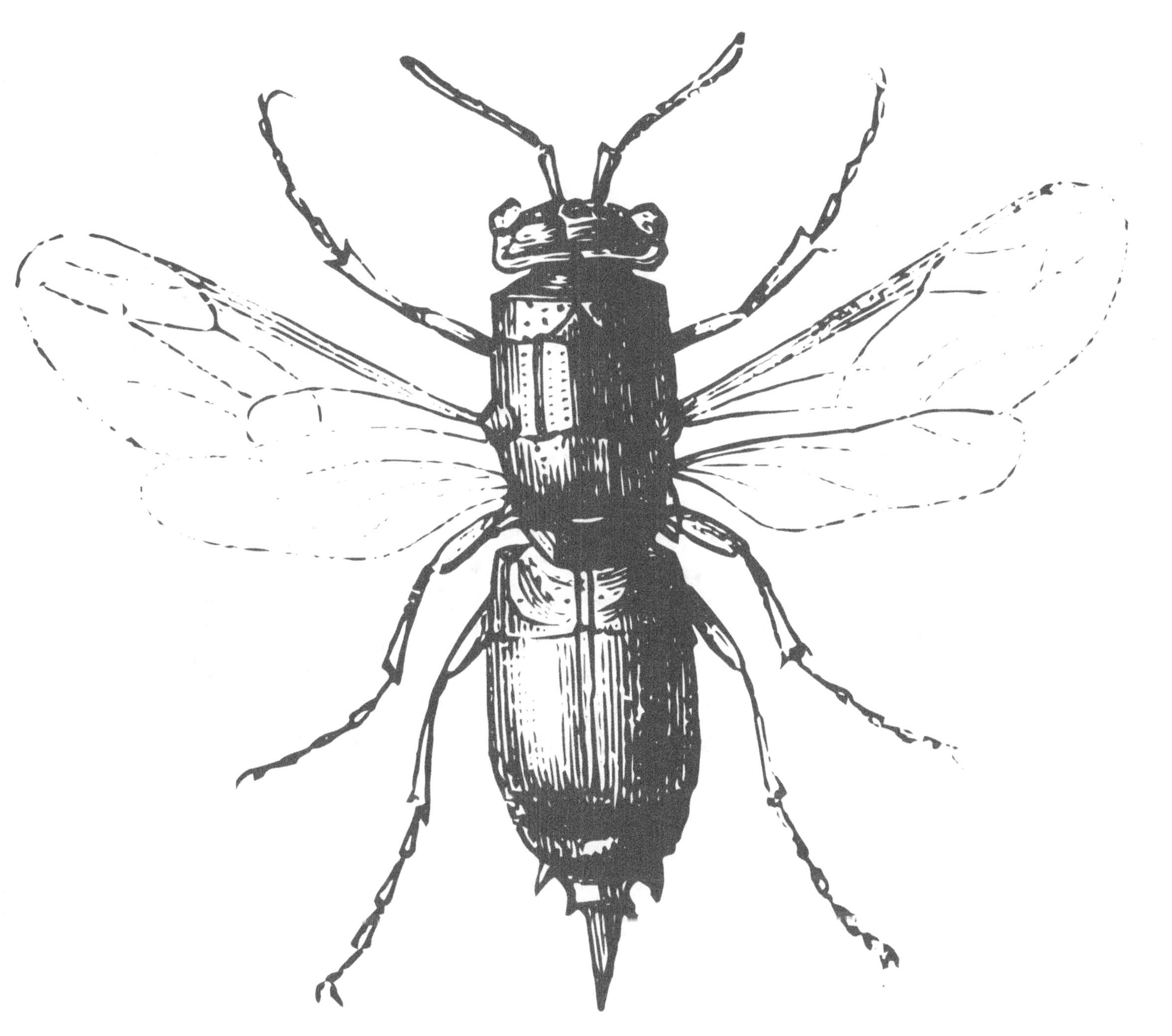

Chrysididae

SUNSET MOTH

COBALT BLUE TARANTULA

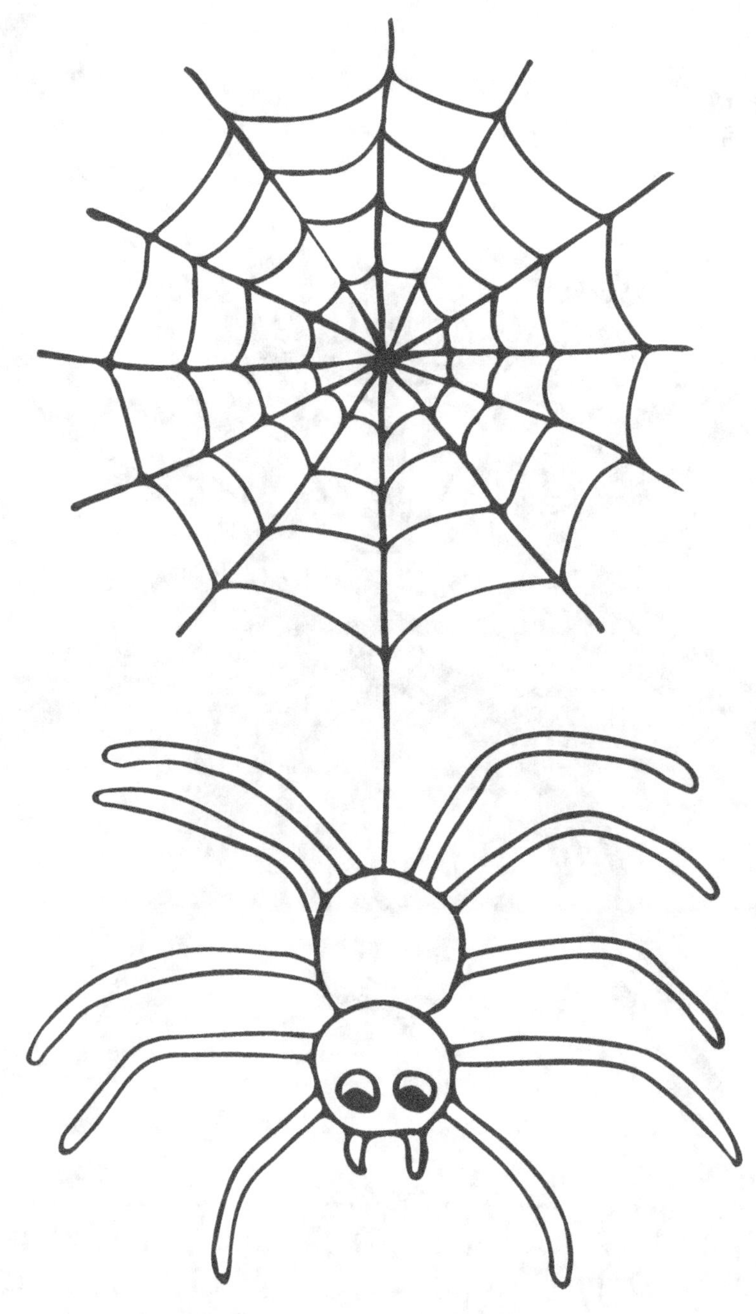

PEACOCK SPIDER

DOGBANE LEAF BEATLE

LILAC BREASTED ROLLER

SCARLET MACAW

ORIENTAL DWARF
KINGFISHER

BLACK BROWED

BARBET

MANDARIN DUCK

GREEN BILLED TOUCAN

KEEL BILLED
TOUCAN

MANDARIN

DRAGONET

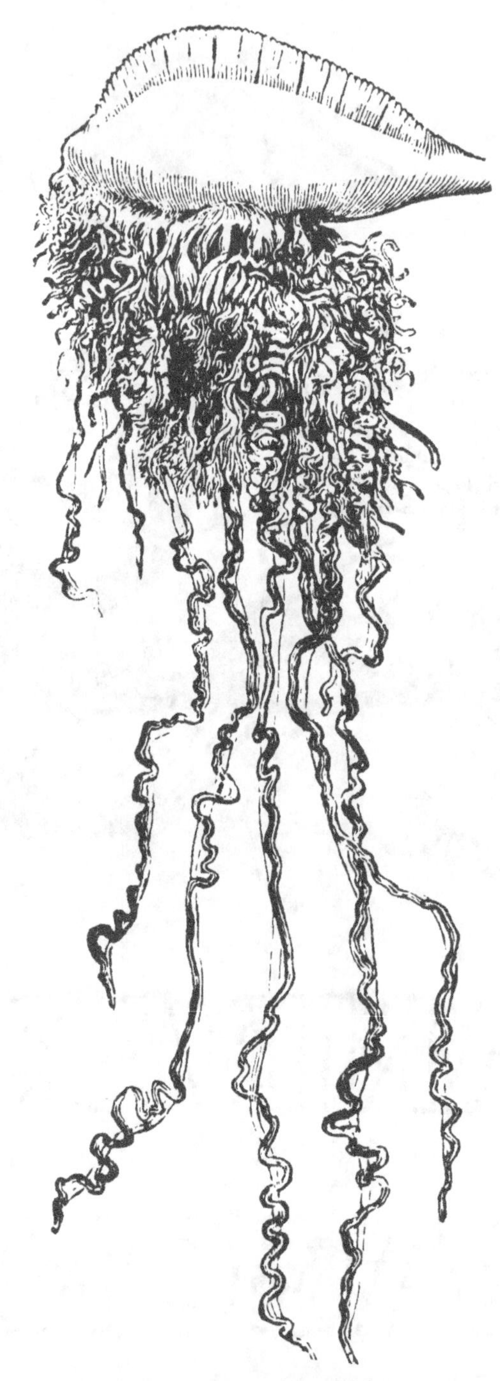

PORTUGUESE MAN OF WAR

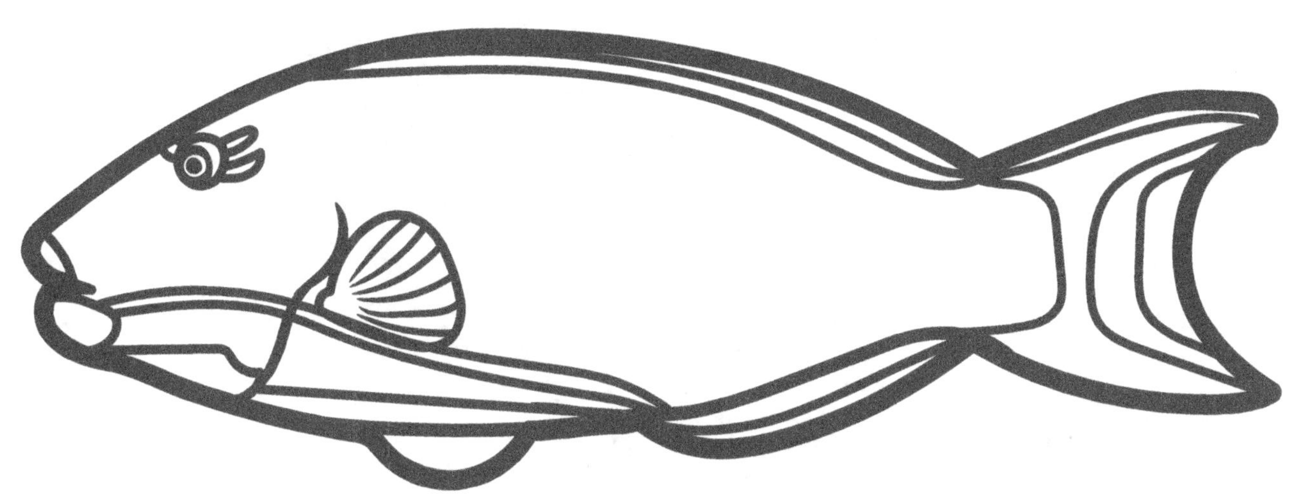

BICOLOR PARROTFISH

PEACOCK MANTIS SHRIMP

LOCH

CHROMODORIS

CEPHEA JELLYFISH

BLUE RINGED

OCTOPUS

PEACOCK

BUTTERFLY